Family Matters
Relationships Matter

DR. VANDANA DESHMUKH

Copyright © 2024 Dr. Vandana Deshmukh

ISBN: 978-1-923078-27-7
Published by Vivid Publishing
A division of Fontaine Publishing Group
P.O. Box 948, Fremantle
Western Australia 6959
www.vividpublishing.com.au

 A catalogue record for this
book is available from the
National Library of Australia

About the Author

Dr. Vandana Deshmukh is a Clinical Psychologist, in Private Practice, in Sydney, Australia

She completed her training in Homeopathic Medicine, from Mumbai, India. She also graduated with a Bachelor of Arts, in Psychology and History, from the University of Mumbai. She then lived as an expatriate, in Oman, for 14 years. She completed her Master of Arts, in History, from the University of Mumbai, via distance education.

In 2002, Vandana migrated to Sydney, Australia. Here, she completed her professional training with a Masters in Clinical Psychology, from the University of Western Sydney (now Western Sydney University), and her PhD, related to Medical Psychology, from the University of Sydney.

Other publications from the author:

Compositions, Creative Words and Travelogue: Journey of Life

www.vividpublishing.com.au/compositions/

Published by Amazon Kindle Direct Publishing

A division of Amazon.com, Inc.

410, Terry Avenue North, Seattle, Washington 98109, U.S.A.

www.amazon.com

Published by the Write Place, Crossword Bookstores, Mumbai, India.

Introduction

Belonging

Relationships and the immediate and extended family are often associated as the most immediate support systems. This is cohesive with the conceptualisation of human beings as social creatures, from the anthropological and existential perspective.

As such the family can be perceived as a team, with the integral team spirit.

In conceptualisation, where individualism has become a prerogative, over the refrain of collectivism, the need for a sense of belonging prevails in many other contexts, as described herewith.

Despite the possible breakdown of family and the associated loneliness, we often see human beings take pride in belonging, to a concept of collectivism, in many formats.

As a child, the individual is a part of a family. This includes parents, siblings and grandparents, in some or most instances, across a spectrum.

This may also include other levels of extended family including aunts, uncles and cousins.

However, the child is also taught to be inclusive, as belonging to an academic institution, including scholastic or sport associated team orientation, of belonging.

The child may often see parents or families belonging to or supporting sports teams and other clubs. This takes a role of pride and solidarity, within the family system.

Belonging to a friend or social circle is also a matter of pride and value.

The role of supporting or belonging to a country, or maintaining dual citizenships, is undoubtedly a universal phenomenon.

As one matures into career hood, the sense of belonging is manifested as belonging to a profession or professional organisation, research body, or the sense of family perception, within an organisation.

In effect, as the child matures to young adult hood, the assumption that the individual operates individualistically is often flawed in argument.

The sense of belonging is often manifested in many aspects, supporting the inherent need for belonging or collectivism.

In the most socially unfavorable situations, unfortunately, individuals breaking away from unsupportive or unhealthy family relationships, may take respite from recluse in belonging to cults or gangs.

The very rare exceptions may be individuals with psychological difficulties, such as social anxiety disorder or a schizoid or schizotypal personality disorder.

Here, reclusive behavior is a manifestation of various traits and integration within a community is a challenge.

However, this is more the exception rather than the rule.

Propagation of families

Traditionally, marriage or the couple dyad perpetuates the family concept across generations.

After a certain age of attaining physical, emotional and sexual maturity, the expectation to find solace in the company of the opposite sex is inherent in most cultures (or same sex in some individuals).

Romantic and companionate linkage becomes an expected norm in most individuals.

A traditional family

Previously, a traditional family may be conceptualised as a joint family, but more recently the trend is towards a nuclear family.

A joint family effectively consists of the patriarch and matriarch and their children and the spouses of the married children and grandchildren.

A nuclear family consists of the parents and their children, till they attain young adulthood.

The grandparents are considered as extended family and aunts, uncles and cousins as associated, extended family.

These perceptions may depend on geographical and cultural expectations.

Monogamy is considered the existing norm in most cultures.

One intimate sexual partner, across the lifespan was the expected preference, especially for females, in some cultures.

However, divorce and remarriage or remarriage, following widowhood, is now an accepted norm.

This healthy trend perpetuates the understanding of the associated psychological difficulties that are inherent to social isolation.

A traditional marriage and changing concepts

In a traditional marriage, the marriage of a couple was arranged previously by the parents.

In more recent times, the male and the female young adults do get the opportunity to meet one another, before finalising the event.

With the opportunities for both males and females to further education and career hood, the concept of romantic marriages is an increasing trend.

Young adults can choose their life partners.

However, early involvement in romantic relationships has its own potential disadvantages with possible excessive peer pressure and distraction from educational and career goals.

The necessity of stability in career options, with a balanced approach towards early relationships, may be recommended.

A heightened focus on appearances and personal attractiveness may take its emotional toll.

Possible emotional immaturity, to handle extremely delicate emotions, is psychologically distressing and damaging.

Additionally,

Inter-caste, inter-regional, inter-racial and international marriages are a trending norm.

There is more diversity in the acknowledgement of common interests.

There is increased viability from the traditional rigid stance of a limited cohort of choice, within caste, religion and racial boundaries.

The increase in cultural diversity and the necessary process of acculturation brings with it inherent advantages.

However, there is an increased need and expectation of social and psychological adjustment, to habits and perspectives.

The motto *love conquers all*, may not be viable unless certain psychological barriers are considered.

Some difficulties may be disruptive to couple harmony.

The propagation of the belief that marriage is a once in a lifetime event is now alleviated by the acceptance of divorce and widowhood, as a sad possibility, that may include remarriage across the life span.

However, maintaining couple harmony where divorce can be avoided, unless recognised as inevitable couple incompatibility, is a reasonable social expectation.

This is especially healthy to the couple and most importantly to the children who are part of this intimate bond of marriage (or of a defacto relationship, as in some couples).

The pros and cons of each conceptualisation discussed above are inherent and fairly individualistic with proponents and opponents of each stance.

The reasons for the proposition or opposition are quite basic but often tangible, intangible or tangential.

The norms and expectations of marriage

In more recent years, ideologies such as the female career, professions, values related to gender roles and diversities are the acknowledged trend.

The underlying concept is that individuals have rights. However, with rights one has roles and responsibilities.

Within rights one has social obligations and anticipated or expected roles and responsibilities.

The concept of responsibilities is prevalent in work ethics too and is integral to the smooth running of any organisation. The organisation may be the microcosm of the family, in some contexts.

Migration to other countries or cultures and associated issues with acculturation may come to the fore, across expected traditions.

Young children in the migrant families may find acculturation especially confronting, during their transition to adolescence and young adulthood.

Maintaining harmony

In conclusion, maintaining harmony, within any relationship, to lead a thriving life, is an essential necessity, requiring adequate insight, awareness and demonstrated effort.

Relationships add joy to life mitigating social isolation and loneliness.

Happy couples, happy families and happy relationships bring with them fulfilled perspectives and contentment.

Therefore, identifying and analysing contentious issues, within an optimistic format of treatment considerations and avenues, is the crux of solving resolvable problems and issues, that undermine psychological wellbeing.

Maintaining Harmony

Specific issues under consideration that may highlight relationship disharmony

Over-enmeshment

The expectations of a marital relationship are often complicated.

There is a spectrum of understanding, often based on the expectation of romantic inclinations as well as companionate affection.

However, unrealistic expectations may often determine couple distress.

The expectation that marriage or a couple dyad means alienation from family, friends or career goals is often a myth.

Over-enmeshment is often as detrimental as disinterest or compromising options of mutual convenience or a symbiotic perspective.

Excessive control and demands can lead to passive resentment and alienation.

The expectation of over-enmeshment is often perpetuated by the psychological need for control, often attributed to low self-esteem or low self-worth.

Other issues may include difficulties with jealousy management, fear of abandonment, or difficulties with goals related to self-actualisation.

Individualistic approaches may complicate issues, especially if one of the partners maintains a high level of individualism.

The pattern of an all-or-none thinking, or an either-or perspective, proves detrimental in most couples.

For example, either a woman accepts marriage in the perspective of a home maker, giving up other career aspirations, or accepts being a career woman, without the expectation of a harmonious long-term relationship.

This is just one example of specific thinking patterns, attributed to difficulties and distress within the couple dyad.

The suggested healthy balance to address issues related to over-enmeshment is the two plus two plus two plus two lifestyle balance, discussed in detail later.

Here, two is specific personal (ME) time, two is couple (US) time, two is family time and two maybe extended family time that is not included in the ME time, as a weekly pattern. This does not include the everyday specific career or homemaker goals.

Career goals, homemaker goals and difficulty with coming to terms with changing expectations

Changes in traditional gender roles, in the area of career goals and homemaker and childcare goals, are often a challenge to couples, open to negotiation and consideration.

The birth of a child and the first two years of infanthood are also challenging and fraught with the need for overarching psychological help.

Postnatal depression or adjustment disorders are incumbent to couple distress.

Whilst postnatal depression is more common in the mother after childbirth, the father may also experience psychological distress, if unsupported during the various competing demands.

Additional help from the extended family including the paternal and maternal grandparents, within a framework of emotional security, is often helpful.

However, individual determination of family as a key resource, maybe the problem issue.

The different perspectives, related to career goals, are as follows.

In the initial scenario, the male is the financial, career or professional determinant and the female in the couple engages in the more traditional homemaker and child-care roles. In very rare instances the roles are reversed.

Often home help or other help such as reliance on take-aways or precooked meals, or dining in a restaurant, is a part of the homemaking process and negotiated accordingly by most couples.

In recent years, with increasing costs and reduced availability of home help and childcare, the reliance on family and extended family is a prerogative.

The division of household chores is often a family con-ference agenda.

Empathy, compassion, mutual understanding, the ability to forgive as also self-compassion, self-care and assertive communication and resilience are the key to any harmonious relationship.

The focus is on behavior change. It is important to focus on goals, rather than personal comments, that could draw a defensive response.

I statements, as defined later, that request behavior change are helpful. The focus is on individual strengths and resources, rather than a constant harping on per-ceived negatives.

In the second scenario, when both the individuals in

a couple have career aspirations and career goals, an equal division of household chores is essential.

Here, maintaining a work-life balance and adequate support from the employment organisation, with realistic expectations, is mandatory.

The expectation that individuals work, over and above the nine-to-five traditional organisational roles, can be challenging.

Shift work adds to the challenge but may often resolve issues like childcare or child education requirements.

Working across time zones, with increased global demands and considerations, are demanding manpower (individual power) and human resources flexibility.

The current trend of some work-from-home days saves travel time, but may be associated with the obvious, inherent organisational challenges.

Certain professions are more challenging than others, requiring additional support from the family front.

In the second scenario, couples are encouraged to make a list of household chores with active and realistic time allocation and equal division and sharing of chores, with alternation in the not so favored chores.

In the third format, both the individuals within the couple dyad are heavily invested in career aspirations, with a complete reliance on home help and childcare help.

However, this is not the most common scenario, demographically.

More recently, the second scenario is the more acknowledged scenario.

Sadly, the fairy tale romance of the Prince Charming, being an overarching provider of all basic requirements, with fiscal fantasy orientations, are inherently conducive to increasing couple distress, with associated disappointments and disillusionments.

Part-time work, job-sharing and organisational flexibility enriches individual life perspective, with focus on career aspirations, family, children and the home, extended family and creative or sports interests.

Maintaining continuity and adequate delineation of roles and responsibilities is necessary.

Financial considerations

The overarching issue in the distribution and allocation of family finances is most adequately determined by inherent family values and the legal system.

Leverage and the associated so-called financial dominance may be considered one of the major challenges related to couple acrimony.

Fiscal and financial cohesiveness is often modeled

across a spectrum of collectivism (as couple related) over individualism..

The understanding of family finances may be conceptualised across varying thought processes.

The first model may include a common forum for all couple earnings.

In this instance, one of the individuals within the couple may be a homemaker, where assets may not be demonstrated as contributed fiscal earnings.

Contributions may however include clever budgeting and management, informed investment habits and sound and astute financial advice and capability.

The mortgages /rents and utilities are paid out of this common pool of assets including children and parent expenses. Savings and future oriented investments are also a prerogative within this model.

The issues with the first model include the possibility of financial dominance from the primary or higher income earner, arbitrary control over spending habits, unequal division of spending assets or constant negotiation about financial conflicts.

The second model includes two income earners, where the couple may decide on paying common utilities, bills and mortgages or rents and children's expenses, as shared. The remainder of the income is at individual disposal for spending and investment.

The above model is a more individualism-oriented model and may feel more autonomous.

However, there could be issues related to anticipated usage of utilities and space, or other such issues, open for potential negotiation.

Also, this model may not account for requirements within the relationship such as unemployment, health issues or other difficulties that involve fiscal collaboration, as a support system.

The third model includes the couple as associated with professional or trading collaboration.

Sole traders or small businesses may include assistance from family members as subsidiary employment.

The fourth model includes collectivistic family models with parents, children and extended family as contributors.

Setting a clear-cut pattern of guidelines here is often helpful, in the more complicated models of collaborative fiscal responsibility.

Expert opinion from financial planners or legal support may be beneficial in some instances.

Conflict within the financial perspective can be a significant source of couple distress and especially so in couples that experience irrevocable incompatibility and the need for financial separation.

Child support and maintenance in families that encounter disharmony and divorce are major psychological challenges.

This is also realistic where remarriages or defacto recoupling can be challenging with children's right to property.

Inherited Assets

Traditionally and legally, currently both the man and woman are equal heirs to parental property and assets. How these assets may be passed on to later generations can be a challenge.

The inheritance rights are often a subject of dissent.

In the more recent prerogative, the legal system encourages equal rights to all siblings over the parental property, also modifiable via the WILL, to a certain extent, but overarchingly maintained by the line of succession.

The assets that are inherited across the line of succession can be considered as from the grandparents to the son or daughter and the grandchildren.

The sons or daughters may decide to utilise the assets

as towards common goals such as immovable property that can be shared by both the son/daughter and grandchild.

In effect, various factors may contribute to disharmony within relationships and information about various skills and strategies, to enhance and maintain relationship harmony, are often of benefit.

Therapeutic Considerations

Understanding the stages of change and motivational incentives within relationships

Relationship issues within dyads (including couples)

Relationships are an integral part of individual functioning and have a considerable contribution in the assessment and evaluation of psychological distress.

Supportive relationships are associated with better psychological outcome. Acrimony in relationships may exacerbate psychological difficulties.

The transtheoretical model, as described ahead, has been explored and validated and applies to the foundation of motivational interviewing and therapy.

However, this model can be elaborated further, within a framework, related to dyads experiencing relationship difficulties.

The relevance is to couples as well as to other relationship interactions.

The stages of change model applies to relationship difficulties adequately.

The model supports in assessing the motivation to change, identifying the pros and cons of change, at every stage, including precontemplation, contemplation, preparation, action and maintenance or relapse prevention.

Stages of change in a romantic or companionate couple relationship

With the current trend, focussing on romantic relationships, over the traditional arranged marriages or marriages of convenience, the process can be assessed as follows.

Initially, individuals meet across a framework of associations and associates including the academic, career or social set-up.

There is a connection or the so-called spark of interest.

The individuals within the dyad may not have decided on being exclusive. They may be involved in the dating process of trying to find the most suitable long-term relationship.

As with the weighing of pros and cons, common interests and deepening attachment, the couple may then decide to be exclusive and move up the next step of the so-called conceptual pyramid.

Engagements are announced, commitment enhanced and consents advocated. This may progress to a defacto relationship.

However, couples may follow the traditional wedding ceremony process, surrounded and blessed by consenting family and friends.

This may progress to a life of matrimony and the expectation of children and family responsibilities.

However, sadly, couples may progress to rejecting or denying exclusivity. This could be for many associated reasons related to contradicting or confusing motivations, jeopardising the concept of monogamy, within the relationship.

This is a very specific challenge to matrimonial harmony and deserves adequate attention and therapy.

The relationship maybe nullified by separation and divorce, depending on contrary motivators.

Relationship difficulties account for psychological distress and are also correlated with significant mental health issues

This includes the experience and management of mood disorders, anxiety disorders, chronic pain and addictive disorders.

Understanding relationships and exploring motivators is, therefore, an important prerogative.

Relationships can be derived within associated changing dynamics and interactions, with exploration of the motivation to change, from one level of intimacy or emotional closeness to another.

These emotional and psychological derivatives include associated or conflictual interactions, within concepts like altruism, sense of responsibility, historical and social perspectives, familial idealism, self-confidence, self-esteem and self-efficacy.

The stages of change within relationship interactions/dynamics is also, often relevant with the social learning theory, contingent to negative and positive reinforcements.

Motivational interviewing strategies and the stages of change model within relationship interactions, may increase the efficacy, if included within the couples therapy paradigm.

This includes addressing ambivalence and the decisional pros and cons analysis. This is also relevant within significant other relationship dyads.

Motivation, to improve relationships within a dyad, is inherent to the intention to engage in therapy, as also inherent to the factors associated with therapeutic change.

The following therapeutic paradigm, within a cognitive behavioural therapy conceptualisation, is not only applicable to relationship distress within the couple dyad but is also applicable to other relationship dyads.

Focus on the relationship is contextual, with both individuals within the dyad accepting the responsibility, to assist a flourishing relationship. This is translated as the metaphorical flowering plant.

Identifying the problem list.

The first stage includes identifying the problem list. The focus is on the modality that behaviour change is possible.

The couples are encouraged to maintain a focus on difficult behaviour, rather than a personal attack, with general statements of inconsiderate, uncaring, or associated characteristic behaviour.

Associated assertive I statements, that focus on a specific behaviour, rather than the person, are encouraged actively.

This includes identifying unacceptable behaviours and negotiable behaviours.

The resistance to change and the associated reluctance is further explored based on the motivators to change behaviour.

The GATE (Goal-Directed Automatic Thoughts Evaluated) model identifies helpful and unhelpful goal directed thoughts.

The strategy including scaling explores whether the behaviour pattern is associated with minimal to maximal interference or impact or subject to modulation (explained in more detail later).

The reasons behind the decision to maximise versus minimise the impact of particular behaviours, on the relationship, are explored.

Associated emotions including anxiety, jealousy, insecurity, low self-esteem, grief and trauma are explored in a frank non-judgmental manner. The focus is on empathy and progressive forgiveness.

Additionally, these relationship difficulties and concomitant therapeutic skills and strategies, are inherent to any meaningful relationship, and not just the couple dyad.

Unacceptable behaviours within a dyad

Negotiable behaviours within a dyad or behaviours that are associated with some distress.

Good aspects within the relationship

Unacceptable behaviours: Each individual in the relationship dyad accepts the responsibility to modify behaviours unacceptable to the other partner. The focus is on the premise that reduction in unacceptable behaviours, will help the relationship flourish.

Negotiable behaviours: Negotiable behaviours are behaviours that may be accepted with some level of couple understanding with increased tolerance and emotional regulation related to any associated distress.

Negotiation within unacceptable behaviours includes anticipation of how difficult the change would be, to the concerned individual. What would change mean? What are the associated levels of resentment?

It is then important to focus on weighing the pros and cons of expected or anticipated change. It is essential to understand the motivators to change.

Change may include altruism, judgement of fairness, balance and mediation.

Change may require management of negative emotions, including jealousy management.

Change may also include accepting responsibility, within a pie of responsibility.

Often one may find that one is approportionating an exaggerated sense of responsibility to the self-experience of negative emotions such as guilt, shame or low self-worth.

However, approportionating overwhelming blame and responsibility to others may include displaced anger, denial and unrealistic expectations of situations or incapacity for cognitive redressal.

The alternative primary concept is that approportionating blame and highlighting blame may not be as constructive as maintaining a sense of collective responsibility, and trying to make amends, or initiating behaviour change where possible.

Acknowledging and accepting circumstantial difficulties and focussing on the ability to make requisite changes is gallant.

When couples create a problem list that includes unacceptable behaviours reaching an impasse, the couple is then encouraged to focus on negotiation as follows (see table).

The more empathetic approach focuses on opening the matter to negotiation.

 Often couples may then identify that it may not be worthwhile in pursuing the behaviour change.

The focus is then on acceptance and focussing on more worthwhile common goals.

Good Aspects or behaviours: The expectation is to focus on the same, especially during the romantic interludes, and in highlighting the positives within the relationship.

Often this communication is pleasing creating a good feeling (similar to endorphins) within the relationship.

Unacceptable behaviour as identified by the partner	
Resentment scaling 1-10 in giving up the unacceptable behaviour	
Associated concerns	
Empathy from the partner towards the level of resentment and assessment of worthwhile demands	
Negotiation towards modifying or mitigating concerns	

Scaling

Scaling often helps identify the interference of problem behaviours, in daily routine.

Scaling also helps couples or relationship dyads decide on whether they would like to minimise the impact of the behaviour, or event under consideration, or maximise it.

This helps develop a prioritisation of the problem list.

However, dyads may decide that they would like to minimise and reflect on the problem behaviour via thought management skills, emotional regulation, anger management, distraction, emotional intelligence and/or empathy.

An assertive statement may resolve the problem behaviour or open it to negotiation.

This is especially so when the behaviour may be an occasional lapse, rather than a recurrent pattern of negative behaviour.

The focus on the bigger picture may be helpful in this exercise.

Concepts like emotional maturity can be a skill of consideration with concomitant attributes or approaches.

Apologies and amends may further alleviate the problem situation. Defining perspectives with clarity and trying to maintain a stance that is appreciative of flexibility, and other perspectives, is helpful.

Thoughts such as "My partner is really hurt and is acting out and would be engaging in a more rational approach soon" may mitigate emotional distress.

Jovial banter may help, however, this needs to be implemented with great care.

This is also true within the therapeutic relationship.

Another definitive concept here is displaced anger. Often the individual may realise that he or she is angry about so many situational life events, and the anger may be deviant or displaced at a person or situation.

Self-awareness and increasing self-realisation certainly helps with examining emotional hyperarousal.

The advantages of employing coping skills and problem-solving strategies may help moderate or mitigate a situational arousal.

Dyads may decide that they would like to maximise on the problem behaviour, including a punitive stance, to rectify the behaviour of concern.

They may include other arbitrators and mediators.

It is important to identify the consequential motivators that maximise determinants within a situation.

Identifying the emotions of concern is often helpful.

Couples/dyads are encouraged to examine critically, the advantages of tangible or intangible leverage, from the problem behaviour occurrence.

Another useful scale is to focus on history and previous conflicts.

Couples or dyads may find that with the improved communication, and a focus on the two plus two plus two plus two balance, in the here and now, may change the outlook on previous difficulties.

Laughter and mirth, used justifiably, within a perspective of empathy, is advocated with care and precaution, as the other individual may feel undermined or misunderstood by misplaced mirth.

When identifying previous problem behaviours, one may utilise the following scale.

When certain behaviours or events happen, they are associated with the feeling of emotional hurt and pain. However, over time one is able to process the impact, and develop a changing perspective.

How much does the previous behaviour/event bother you now?

Not at all   A little   Moderately

Very much   Couldn't be worse

The higher reactivity indicates unprocessed emotions, that need prioritisation in the treatment process.

Often couples/dyads are requested to focus on the time together, within a sense of homeostasis, leaving complicated processing and conflictual differences to the therapy session.

This instils increasing confidence, in the experience of normalcy, within the relationship.

This also helps identify any defining need to exacerbate conflict within the relationship, and any underlying motivators or destructive behaviour patterns, including complex personality traits.

Attention seeking behaviours, undermining behaviours, and the need to define the creative self within the self-actualisation process, are important issues for consideration.

Relationships and helpful strategies

Initially, validation of expectations and the ability to find good reasons for emotions, or behaviour, is often helpful.

The good reasons paradigm is often helpful, in helping the significant other, in the relationship, feel sufficiently understood.

Trying to assess and initiate behaviour change or changes within the relationship is helpful.

The focus is on the anticipated behaviour change and not the concerned individual.

Direct confrontational statements are inadequate and encounter defensiveness.

Stages of change in behaviour elaborated within the concept of change of unacceptable behaviours:

According to this model, individuals progress through different stages of change as they adopt a change in their behavior or outlook.

The first stage is precontemplation in which persons do not communicate any willingness to change.

During the second stage of contemplation, persons slowly become aware of and begin thinking seriously about their problems.

The third stage, preparation, is associated with persons voicing a commitment to change behaviour, or the way of doing or experiencing or perceiving things, in the near future.

The fourth stage action depicts persons, who have been actively pursuing changes, for several months.

Maintenance is the fifth stage, in which the achieved changes persist, for a longer time.

Persons in the termination stage have permanently changed their behaviour.

Alternatively, there may be a relapse back to the previous unhelpful ways of doing experiencing or perceiving things.

It is known that people may move to and fro between these various stages of behaviour change.

However, it is important to realise that one can maintain the ongoing helpful change in behaviour or outlook, via certain motivational strategies.

These include weighing the advantages and disadvantages of behaviour, or outlook change, and efforts to maintain the same.

For some, it may mean consolidating previously achieved gains.

Treatment does focus on setting goals, or identifying what people would like to change, about the way they do things.

Treatment focuses on strategies that would help dyads make these changes.

Assess difficulties and try to focus on shared common goals

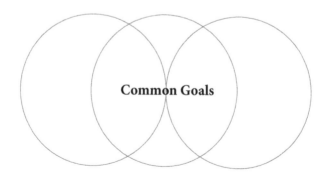

Focusing on common goals often helps the relationship flourish despite differences.

The premise is that, even identical twins, with the similar genetic material, often act and behave differently, and respond differently, to environmental feedback.

Hence, the expectation that individuals, within the couple or any other relationship dyad, would think or behave in exactly the same way, to all environmental challenges, within the internal and external milieu, is often unrealistic.

The more realistic expectation is that dyadic agreement could be perceived in many, or most situations.

However, often individuals may agree to disagree, in some instances, accepting difference of opinion openly, and as inadvertent.

However, common goals help foster togetherness and cohesiveness.

Common goals may include the romantic feeling, desirability, companionship, teamwork and similar interests, within a couple relationship.

Often having children, building a home, having a pet, common assets, professional or business interests, are recognised common goals.

Altruism, family history of joyful memories, laughter

and mirth may also keep couple and other relationships healthy.

Premise of cognitive behavioural concepts

Does the way we think, affect the way we feel, and behave?

<u>YES</u>

Imagine a friend walking towards you. Instead of smiling and speaking, your friend walks past you, without even acknowledging you.

What might you think about this behaviour?

If you think that your friend is angry or upset with you, then you might feel anxious or depressed.

If you think that your friend is stressed by something and did not notice you, then you might feel very little emotion, or perhaps even feel compassion for your friend.

In other words, emotions are strongly influenced by thoughts, assumptions, underlying beliefs or our expectations and interpretations of the situation.

Different people, often have very different thoughts and therefore reactions, in response to the same event.

For example: Three people are waiting at a bus stop. They see the bus, hail the bus and it just drives by, without stopping.

The first person gets angry and clenches his/her fists.

The second person gets anxious and his/her heart starts to pound.

The third person shrugs his/her shoulders and gets on with reading the newspaper.

The same event produced three different responses because it was not the event that directly produced the feelings and behaviour, but the thoughts the three people had about the event.

What might people have thought?

The first person might have thought, "That driver should have stopped. Now I'm going to be late for an important meeting."

The second person might have thought, "I'm going to be late; I'll never get everything done in time and the rest of the day will be a disaster."

The third person might have thought, "I might be late but there's not much I can do about it".

How would that make them feel?

If you are like the first or second person you might

tend to see things as worse than they need to be and you may cause yourself unnecessary worry.

Distress is often caused when people expect the worst to happen.

Unhelpful thoughts such as

"I know that something dreadful is going to happen"

"Everyone will see I'm not coping"

"I really don't think I will be able to do it" are often automatic and they affect how you behave and how distressed you become in situations.

These thinking patterns are habits and as such can be changed.

The first step is to identify the thoughts. The questions to ask are:

What was going on in my mind before I started to feel distressed?

What does this mean to me?

What images or memories did I have in this situation?

Can we identify helpful vs. unhelpful thinking?

Often people describe their thinking in terms of positive or negative thinking. However, these terms can be misleading.

For example, thinking positively could result in ignoring your relationship concern and hoping that it will go away.

In this case, thinking positively will not be helpful in sorting out the problem. So, thinking too positively can amount to denying the problem.

Negative thinking is similar to positive thinking, in that, it too could be inaccurate, but in the opposite direction.

So, thinking negatively could mean that you think nothing will ever be any better.

Such thoughts are likely to be obstacles to your attempt to improve the situation.

It can, therefore, be more useful to talk about helpful thinking versus unhelpful thinking.

Helpful ways of thinking are those that enable you to deal effectively with a problem or a source of stress.

Helpful thinking may not solve all problems, but it should allow you to make some progress.

In contrast, unhelpful ways of thinking are those that cause you even more distress.

Helpful thinking helps reduce the level of distress experienced.

Further, we can identify some of the common mistakes or errors in thinking, or unhelpful thinking.

Often, these thoughts are automatic and one needs to engage in the effort, to identify the thoughts, assumptions, underlying beliefs or our expectations and interpretations of the situation, that are related to our distress.

Unhelpful thinking

It is possible that we may engage in unhelpful thinking.

Processing thinking patterns may abate heightened emotions.

Thought: *My partner and I should agree on everything.*

Possible unhelpful thinking error:

Polarised thinking where an experience is viewed in either/or terms with no shades of grey.

Thought: *My partner should understand my needs, without me having to tell them.*

Possible unhelpful thinking error:

Setting unrealistic expectations or living by fixed rules of how you or the others should behave.

One may also set unrealistic expectations that may not fit the current situation.

One may feel excessive distress when these expectations are not met, or the rules are changed.

Thought: *Other people are more fortunate than me.*

Possible unhelpful thinking error:

<u>Selective thinking</u>

This includes filtering out the positives, dwelling on one unpleasant event and dismissing all the pleasant things.

This includes focussing on evidence that supports your negative view and disregards evidence that does not.

This pattern of thinking disregards prior coping skills.

There is a disregard for prior ability to cope with difficult situations.

Thought: *My partner tried to help me to make me feel inadequate*

Possible unhelpful thinking error:

Converting positives into negatives by not giving yourself or others credit for talents, achievements or concern.

Thought: *My partner never does any household chores.*

Possible unhelpful thinking error:

Overgeneralising

If it happened once, it would happen again, with the expectation that if things have gone wrong in the past, they will continue to do so.

Thought: *I am responsible to maintain all harmony within the relationship. I should be passive at all times.*

Possible unhelpful thinking error:

Personalising: It is all my fault

Taking responsibility and blame for anything unpleasant and feeling distressed.

Taking responsibility for other people's feelings and actions and forgetting that they are ultimately in control of their lives.

Thought : *I will never cope with my relationship difficulties, at a social event.*

Possible unhelpful thinking error:

Jumping to conclusions

Making assumptions and possibly negative or un-helpful predictions.

Most often, you will discover that what you had feared, never happened.

Thought: *I will never achieve any of my goals because of my relationship difficulties.*

Possible unhelpful thinking error:

Blowing situations out of proportion

Believing that events are more catastrophic, than they really are.

The mistake in thinking includes jumping to conclusions about negative events and blowing situations out of proportion.

Can we challenge our thoughts? How can we challenge un-helpful thinking?

To change thinking patterns, to more helpful thinking, one can treat thoughts as guesses and not facts.

One can then develop more realistic beliefs by consid-ering all of the evidence and by obtaining additional information where necessary.

The questions to ask are

Is this thought realistic?

What is the evidence for and against the thought?

Am I making one of the thinking errors listed above?

Is this thinking helpful?

If not, is there a better helpful way of assessing the situation?

Can I engage in more helpful goal-directed thinking?

Also, it is important to identify the thoughts, assumptions, underlying beliefs or our expectations and interpretations of the situation, that are related to our distress by asking

What does this thought that is related to the distress mean to me?

<u>And then</u>

What is the evidence for and against this interpretation?

What are the advantages and disadvantages of this interpretation?

Is my thinking interpretation goal-directed?

Why is writing down your thought management important?

Writing down the situation, thoughts and emotions and thought challenge, in the thought management record, is helpful.

This helps us deal with our thoughts and emotions in a structured manner.

The thought challenges that we use remain a resource to deal with future similar unhelpful thinking, in other situations.

Unhelpful thinking includes thinking that situations are insufferable or catastrophic, when in actuality they are not.

However, sometimes the thoughts maybe factual.

It is then important to identify what the thought means to us.

It is also important to identify associated schemas or long-term patterns of thinking and interpretations.

It is important to assess past memories, that revoke an active, distressed emotional response, in similar situations or experiences.

It is important to then focus on problem solving and assessing the pros and cons of each aspect of the response to the situation.

It is also important to identify goals and to focus on thinking patterns that are goal-directed .

Goal-Directed Automatic Thought Evaluation (GATE)

Goal	
Automatic Thought	
Emotion	
Behaviour	
Alternative Goal-directed Thought	

Core Beliefs and Schemas

I am

Others are

The world is

Relationship balance: the two plus two plus two paradigm

This paradigm helps individuals flourish within a relationship, by channelising an adequate balance, across the spectrum of an individual's perspective and perceived requirements.

This paradigm assists depolarisation and enriches life experiences.

The individual tries to achieve a balance of two as specific personal (ME) time, two is couple (US) time, two is family time and two maybe extended family time, that is not included in the ME time, as a weekly pattern.

This does not include the everyday specific career or homemaker goals.

Personal time is the ME time, couple time is the US time and family time includes the time spent as parents and children.

Extended family time includes maternal and paternal grandparents and other extended family.

As a balanced lifestyle, couples or dyads are encouraged to retain significant, prior support relationships, including parents, siblings and extended family, individual friends and collegiate relationships, as ME time.

The ME time is an opportunity to pursue interests and hobbies.

It is also an opportunity for individuals to focus on the concept that activities can be enjoyed, within the perspective of the self.

This also encompasses activities that one can enjoy, without the necessary constraint of needing perpetual or constant companionship.

The other individual in the couple dyad is also encouraged to have an enriched ME time.

This helps overcome issues related to mistrust, fear of abandonment, jealousy or generalised issues with self-actualisation and goal setting.

With the current increase in the rate of couple divorce, and expectations of individualism in approaches, having a significant ME identity is psychologically healthy.

This helps with associated distraught emotions or feelings, should irrevocable differences mitigate couple harmony.

However, the most helpful aspect, that maintains couple harmony, is a strong inclination and effort, in maintaining a quality US time.

This is the romantic time where couples put aside differences and try to plan and develop patterns of romantic interludes.

Sexual intimacy also perpetuates the couple closeness. This varies across a spectrum of individual perspectives.

However, not every romantic interlude is expected to end in physical intimacy. The focus is on emotional closeness and connection.

Couples are advised to reminisce on happy interactions and fun moments and common areas of interest.

The attempt to avoid boredom, monotony and neglect of the nurture of a relationship, is inherent.

The US time also is an opportunity for couples to experience the concept that they can spend quality time together that is devoid of conflict, argument, difference of opinion, and any existing troubled marital situation.

Couples are often advised to leave the discussion of conflict and unacceptable situations to the therapy session.

The couple can hence maintain a sense of homeostasis, learning to postpone conflicts, maintaining emotional regulation and retaining efforts to maintain congenial and respectful stances, within the relationship.

This is also an opportunity for the children within the family to spend time with the grandparents, both paternal and maternal.

Healthy, congenial, secure attachment is the key over excessive enmeshment.

Additionally, afterschool hobbies and sport activities maintain a balance within child education, sports, arts and social opportunities.

The family time includes the time spent as a family, including parents and children.

Infants and toddlers may, of course, require additional consideration and individual attention from family.

Even so, the couples are encouraged to focus on finding optimal ME and US time, despite the challenges of having children.

The extended family time is parents, children and extended family, over and above any ME time.

This can be extended family related to oneself and/ or extended family related to the partner, in a couple dyad.

A partner can choose to be adequately involved, in the care and support of the extended family, related to the other partner.

This can foster closeness and harmony and may enhance many happy, associated memories, for the couple.

However, sometimes taking the more secondary or supportive role maybe helpful, based on individual requirements and time constraints.

Often, a helpful spouse/partner may act as an intermediary, without seeking overwhelming attention, depending on situational prerogatives.

Each couple/dyad may have individual difficulties

and perception of resources in implementing the above strategies.

These difficulties are addressed on an individual basis, via individual prerogatives.

Jealousy Management

As with anxiety, sadness, guilt and anger, jealousy can be an emotion of concern affecting social, occupational and relationship functioning.

Jealousy, as an associated symptom, is not specific to a mental health condition.

However, jealousy can be a source of major psychological distress.

Acceptance that some jealousy is normal, is the key to self-awareness.

However, jealousy can become an emotion of concern.

Jealousy may also be associated with low self-esteem.

Jealousy maybe associated with core beliefs of entitlement.

Jealousy maybe associated with nagging resentment.

Jealousy maybe related to a person (specific) or generalised.

However, emotions of jealousy are manageable, mitigating the associated psychological distress.

Mitigating jealousy may include specific self-modification skills and relationship enhancement skills.

Thought Management and common thinking errors related to jealousy

Polarised Thinking

Catastrophic Thinking

Focusing on the negatives and marginalising the positives

Setting unrealistic expectations or living by fixed rules

Overgeneralising

Helpful Self-Statements

Appreciating the qualities that one may feel jealous about and setting small goals of self-achievement.

Working on self-esteem and self-confidence with focus on three good qualities about self, on an ongoing basis, in daily activities

Feeling gratitude

Practising empathy

Exposure to jealousy causing situations, acceptable within the limits of the relationship

Enhancement of security within the relationship over insecure attachment by strengthening the US time of the relationship

Inbuilt resilience and consideration to appreciation of various achievements, despite adverse situations or life events, is helpful.

Strategies of negotiation and mediation to manage resentment.

This includes an understanding of the other person's perspective and prerogative.

This also includes trying to identify controlling patterns of behaviour, that may have a basis in insecure attachments, fear of abandonment or issues with self-esteem.

Exploring and introspecting on an inadequate quality of ME time, or inability in finding contentment within an enriched ME time, may help resolve some of the issues with emotion regulation.

Family Relationships and Communication

Communication styles

Being Passive means:

Not saying what you want

Valuing the needs of others above your own

Avoiding dealing with difficult situations

Apologising for things that are not your fault

Letting others impose their views on you

Blaming yourself for things that aren't your fault

Being Aggressive means:

Imposing your views on others

Wanting to win at all costs

Not listening to what others have to say

Disregarding the rights of others

Intimidating or belittling others

Being prepared to use force to get what you want

Making unreasonable demands

Assertiveness is NOT being passive and NOT being aggressive.

Assertiveness means:

Believing in yourself

Being honest about your feelings

Clearly stating the facts

Acknowledging the rights of others

Listening to other peoples' points of view

Negotiating

Compromising

Being in control of your behaviour.

Communicating with I statements and avoiding You statements.

The **I** statement is a way of communicating how another person's actions affect you, without escalating conflict.

Rather than making judgments about the other person, you are telling them how their actions affect you, how you feel and why.

In this instance, it might be important to focus on a specific behaviour that you would like to see changed, instead of a general negative statement about the person.

Then, you can tell them what you want or need to happen in the future, and, if necessary, what you will do in response.

These are the three, or maybe four steps in the I statement process

"I feel..."

Make an honest statement about how you are feeling.

For example: *I feel very angry right now..."*

"because..."

Tell the person what action or behaviour of theirs has triggered your feelings.

For example: *because you did not pick me up when you said you would*

"consequences..."

and I ended up going late to the doctor's appointment."

"I want or need..."

Behaviour change expected.

For example: *I need you to be on time in the future. If you have to change plans, I would like you to call me.*

Accepting amends for any perceived hurtful behavior

is the way forward, to onward strengthening of relationships.

However, often despite amends and positive behavior change, ongoing healing of rifts may be related to unhelpful agendas and motivators, that do not focus on strengthening the family ties.

The pros and cons of unhelpful agendas and divisive leverage is often based on unresolved resentments and negative evaluation of the family dynamics.

It is important to address these agendas in a constructive manner. Apologies and amends are a strong motivator to maintain ongoing harmony. Negotiation is the key to resolving the situations.

Issues of dissent such as household chores and routines, managing social interactions and balancing many requisite commitments, focuses on aspects of emotional intelligence.

Anger Management

Anger is generally related to rules or expectations, that one may have, about significant others, or situations.

When these rules are not met, one may experience anger, as an emotion.

This feeling maybe associated with angry thoughts, alienation, disassociation, overcontrolling behaviour, disrespectful behaviour, verbal abuse, emotional abuse or at times, physical abuse.

It is necessary to identify anger, as early warning signs, before it escalates to conflict. This includes angry thoughts, raised voice, redness of face and other such signs of hyperarousal.

Calling for time out from the situation, or argument or discussion, is essential.

If an individual, within a relationship, calls for time out, it is helpful, if this is respected by the other individual.

Practising relaxation and other calming or self-soothing strategies is necessary.

Considerate, responsible and emphatic thought processes may assist situations.

Identifying and addressing underlying, unresolved dissent, is indicated.

Conflict Management Guidelines

Set aside some time to discuss the topic

Start the discussion when you both feel calm

Call for time out, if emotions begin to escalate, and set a time to return to the   discussion

Alternate roles of speaker and listener but let only one person have the floor at a time.

Speaker

State how you see the problem (define it clearly)

Focus on the problem not the person

Use I statements

Listener

Listen and avoid judging what the speaker says

Ask questions to clarify and further your understanding

When both of you have said your point of view, come to an agreement as to what the problems are.

Brainstorm solutions

State which solutions you would both be willing to try.

Agree on one solution that meets both your needs.

Strategies to deal with criticism.

Be COURTEOUS in your approach

Do not use verbal threats or physical attacks.

Self-calming statements: "Don't take it personally" "You are better than that"

Distraction: Distract yourself with another activity such as riding your bike, cleaning the house, reading a book.

Humour: Try and find something funny about the situation or yourself

Rationalising: "If I were him what would I be thinking or feeling; maybe she/ he has a right to be angry"

Self-praise: "I did a really good job staying calm, it was tough but I did it"

Assertiveness allows you to express your unhappiness with the situation, without losing control.

Stress and Resources: Eustress and Distress

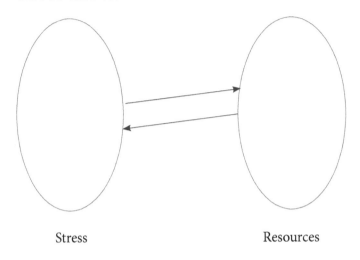

Stress   Resources

When stress and resources are well aligned an individual would experience eustress, or stress that is sufficiently challenging and balanced, increasing functioning and performance.

When stress and resources are not well aligned, an individual would experience distress, or stress that is not optimal to functioning and performance.

It is helpful then to optimise resources or to try to revise/reduce stressors.

Resources can be related to self, to significant others, clinicians or even optimal medication use.

Mitigating stress can involve but is not limited to stress management or time management strategies, including planning, prioritising and problem solving.

63

Often the expectation in any relationship dyad is that the other individual in the dyad, is a resource, to mitigating stress.

This enhanced perception of the individual, is associated with a positive feeling, within the relationship.

However, if the partner or the relationship dyad is perceived as enhancing stress, instead of mitigating stress, then the relationship maybe perceived as conflicted.

This could be a fair or unfair perception, or displaced anger and resentment.

Enhancing the feeling of wellbeing within the relationship

Often a couple in distress will focus on the negatives and on previous negative events.

The couple or the relationship dyad is then advised to make it a routine:

To highlight three nice aspects of the relationship

To focus on three appreciated behaviours during the day

Avoid generalising and judgemental statements.

Focus on behaviour change.

Often common goals and appreciation of the other person's prerogatives and priorities and maintaining support to contingencies, is helpful

Involvement and approval of cherished activities is an adequate forum of togetherness.

Self-Esteem, Self-Worth and Locus of Control

Often issues with low self-esteem and low self-worth, may complicate relationships.

It is important to focus on self-esteem by highlighting appreciable qualities, about self.

Translating these qualities to behaviours identified during the day, reflecting perceived positives, is necessary.

Positive affirmations about the self are helpful.

Feelings of self-efficacy, within realistic expectations and goals, is worthwhile.

If the goals are too easy, the experience of achievement is modest.

If goals are too demanding or unrealistic or are considered an imposition, then the achievement of goals is a struggle, and maybe demoralising and tiresome.

Setting realistic and achievable goals and challenges, enhances feelings of self-efficacy and self-worth.

The concept of the locus of control is derived from health psychology.

Locus of control may also refer to a person's beliefs about how much potential they have, to modify what happens to them, in their life.

This may also be related to the perception of how much influence they have, over what happens in the world around them.

The three concepts in health psychology are the internal locus of control, where health may be attributed to factors such as self-determination, of a healthy lifestyle.

The external locus of control includes the belief that health is attributed to powerful others (such as one's doctor).

The chance locus of control includes factors such that health and well-being is attributed to chance or luck factors, outside ones control.

These individuals may experience inadequacy in managing their health issues and often express poor quality of life and health management.

They may hence, experience higher levels of anxiety and depression, as comorbid to the medical condition.

The concept of the locus of control has been well identified in improving quality of life, in individuals experiencing chronic medical conditions, such as asthma, diabetes mellitus or hypertension.

These concepts seem meaningful in the management of emotions, within relationships.

This is especially true in issues related to self-worth and self-esteem.

Individuals, experiencing an internal locus of control, believe that the outcomes of their actions are results of their own abilities, or are self-determined.

Their concepts about self include confidence in their abilities and self-compassion and self-care.

These individuals do not take affront easily and evaluate the situation with calm maturity.

Often the dictum of serenity, in wanting to change the issues that can be changed, identifying or accepting the issues that cannot be changed, and finding the wisdom to evaluate the difference, signifies emotional wellbeing.

However, the commitment to self-actualisation and meaningful goals, is necessarily demonstrated adequately.

Often hurtful or painful behaviour from significant others, may be viewed through the calm lens of empathy.

For example, thoughts such as "This person must be hurting a lot himself or herself to act out in this manner" fosters a sense of empathy and care, mitigating focus on individual hurt.

These individuals believe in their self-actualisation goals, their abilities and their sustained performance.

They are self-aware of their potential and previous, positive outcomes.

They also believe that every action has its consequence, which makes them accept the fact that events happen, however, that it is up to them to develop adequate responses.

This, in addition to a realistic pattern of appraisal and evaluation of behaviour, assists them with adequate emotional regulation and focus on goal-directed activity and common goals.

Individuals with an external locus of control, attribute outcomes of events, to external circumstances.

Individuals with an external locus of control maybe compliant, or often over dependent.

They may have difficulty in being assertive, and may manage conflicts passively, or may portray the victim role, in some instances.

They may experience low self-esteem and low self-worth, leaving them vulnerable to negative influences, with limited distress tolerance.

They may develop social anxiety with a fear of negative evaluation and over compensatory behaviours.

An individual with a chance locus of control believes in factors such as fate, luck, history, and the influence of powerful forces.

The associated belief is that the world is too complex, for one to predict or influence its outcomes.

Again, they may experience issues in relationships, with passive aggressive attitudes.

This could include complications such as anxiety or depression, in maintaining quality of life.

Resolving issues related to self-esteem, self-worth and an internal locus of control, with self-awareness, may mitigate many relationship issues.

Assets Management and Financial Autonomy

Assets are an integral aspect of every family situation. Managing assets can be a source of stress and result in extensive mediation requirements.

Within a couple relationship, the expectation is that the family earnings are divided equally between the couple.

Financial separation includes disclosure of all couple assets and a distribution of assets, within the legal framework, and within prior agreements and under-standings, if any.

However, in essence, if a couple does dissolve the rela-tionship, it often leaves the children, within the family perspective, devoid of property rights or demonstrable tangible assets.

Step-parents and step-children and half-children, often complicate the right to parent or inherited property.

This is addressed legally to a certain extent; however, the issue is open to dissent, contention and psycholog-ical stress.

The following suggestions are mediatory in perspec-tive, with the aim of easing contention.

However, these suggestions are open to individual negotiation, within the prerogative of child rights and responsibilities, within the family perspective.

With the given involvement of children and expecta-tions in homemaker management, it seems fair that the children are considered equal stakeholders, in the family earnings.

In essence, if a family consists of two parents and two children, the family earnings could be divided by four, with some portion going to the parent home, which is often under joint parent names.

It is possible that some portion goes to child expenses, common household bills and common holidays.

Accounting parent expenses and future parent savings, the balance can be equally divided between all four stakeholders.

This can be invested as common assets or immovable property, that can be accessible as assets, to both the parent and the child.

The child is an integral aspect of the family system and contributes to the family well-being, in many different ways.

The adolescent or the young adult may take on many homemaker roles, and may often assist in the development, maintenance and investment of many family assets, via innovative ideas and manpower (individual power).

Additionally, the child has the right to inheritances from the grandparents, where these inheritances may be acknowledged into immovable property or assets. The investments could be demonstrably contributory, to both the child and parent.

Whilst the legal and social system works well in most instances, there are examples where the legal system may not prove adequate, in fairness.

Legalities do not become the overarching issue.

The focus is on developing a realistic and a rational understanding of individual requirements and a healthy, comfortable and reasonably recreative lifestyle.

The focus is on belonging and collectivistic considerations over individual gain and disruption of the family modality.

Another issue, that is not addressed legally, but is often the source of couple distress and consideration, is parental expectations from children, in sustaining lifestyle after retirement.

Parents often invest heavily in the children's education or in providing support to develop professions, business or immovable and tangible assets.

Here, the right to parent support, in ageing years, from sons and daughters, can be an issue of contention.

The issues related to loneliness and social isolation, and financial support to maintain extended family connectivity, and recreative goals, is an issue that recommends humanistic and collectivistic considerations, over legal prerogatives.

Individualistic approaches often fail to address the above issues.

These are often negotiated within the couple perspective, with the aim of achieving fairness.

The evaluation of perspective, within the neutral framework of the psychological therapy process, is often beneficial in the mediation process.

Should a couple decide on a financial separation/ divorce, then the child (in a family of four), has the right to claim the one fourth section of the joint assets, in the form of immovable property, or as tangible assets in joint names.

Concepts of proportionality and percentage

Concepts such as proportionality and percentage may be of utility, to manage major difference in the income or assets, of the two individuals, within a dyad.

For example, in a couple relationship, if one partner pays 20 % of his/her income as rent, it may be empathic and considerate to expect that the other partner also pay 20 % of his/her income as rent.

This means that the actual amount paid by the two individuals, in the couple dyad, may be entirely different, but dependent on percentage value, of the income earned.

The same can be upheld when purchasing gifts or planning events.

For example, an individual earning AUD 4000/- may purchase a gift worth AUD 100/-.

The second individual may be earning AUD 2000/- and could say purchase a gift worth AUD 50/-.

However, in cost effect and value of contribution, generosity and thoughtfulness, the two individuals are experiencing the same level of altruism.

This concept is also helpful when individuals are stressed, over celebrated events, like the festive season, or birthdays or wedding anniversaries.

In effect, this concept takes away the stress of competition, and any awkwardness on festive events. This concept helps individuals feel liberated, at being understood, on the basis of realistic expectations.

Individuals could find added value, at their attendance of events, in a valued and refreshing manner, without any possible negative labeling.

The contribution by percentage and proportion is amenable to problem solving and fair resolution.

However, disposable or cash flow income, versus accrued or invested income and tangible versus intangible assets, are additional concepts that add to the complexity of the issue, leaving the definers open to negotiation.

The underlying emphasis is on empathy building and flexibility in the rationale of thinking patterns.

Other specific issues

Care of the children within the family

Care of the children within the family

Children and parenthood are extremely joyful and desired experiences.

The inbuilt desire towards procreation, is the best expression, of the feeling of fulfillment, in most individuals.

However, bringing up children is stressful, and especially so, in the first two years.

Following two infant and toddler years, the child is able to articulate and express opinions and requests, in a much more coherent manner.

Communication between parents and children, is the most essential requisite, of the relationship.

The focus on safe play over impulsiveness and arbitrary exploration and hyperactivity from the child, is most essential.

Developmentally appropriate challenges, with gradual increase in independence and autonomy, are crucial.

Often, the mother maybe the primary caregiver or nurturer.

However, fathers are increasingly involved, in parental care.

This is also especially so when both couples have career goals.

Couples may then experience a difference of opinion, in some basic aspects of childcare. This may be related to their own positive and negative experiences, during their upbringing.

Often these differences are resolved, through mutual understanding and behavioural experiments, over what works best for the child.

Having neutral guidance from health professionals or well-evaluated and researched self-help books, may be helpful.

Weighing the pros and cons, based on availability of resources, potential necessity and common perspectives, are often helpful.

Children with special needs, may have additional requirements, and may need more objective assistance.

The right age to send the infant to childcare is often debatable. This often, depends on individual requirements, and individual circumstances.

Planning, prioritising and problem solving are necessary skills, in maintaining harmony

The extended family often, also plays an integral role in child development and child self-worth.

Treating both maternal and paternal grandparents fairly, helps instil the ideas of fairness, within the child perspective.

The percentage and proportion idea works well, if both sides of the extended family, are unequal in asset accrual.

It is important to communicate to the child, to appreciate the love, affection and sense of belonging, that extended family brings to the child environment, helping child development, well into maturity and adulthood.

Cohesiveness of ideology, over conflicting interactions, is often helpful.

The parents may take on more leadership roles, however, the willingness to lend an ear to helpful advice and suggestions, that are borne out of experience, is a valuable exercise.

Intrinsic values such as respect for everyone, learning to share, being helpful, politeness, good hygiene, waiting for your turn in communication and demands, developing a sense of fairness and empathy, are valued qualities.

However, the overarching issue is to communicate adequately with the child, with the focus on child safety.

The key is to focus on individual strengths and choices, from an adaptive perspective.

The child is an extremely important and beloved contributor to the family dynamics, in most instances.

In later years, children are expected to help within the home situation, within a developmental perspective.

Providing additional, objective rationale to children, focused on understanding family requirements, is obviously helpful.

Communication, based on respecting family commitments, within the increasing developmental need for autonomy, is often critical.

Additionally, gaining support and resources, within the extended family dynamics, adds to the perception of collectivistic joys, in shared family requirements and recreation.

Extended family may help with childcare, child education or afterschool care and activities, in various negotiated formats.

Essential communication and negotiation, with adequate planning and consideration, goes a long way in skilled management.

Disrespect, meanness to other children, bullying, groupism and ostracism, based on unrealistic assessments by parents or peers, is often undesirable socially and psychologically.

Postpartum or postnatal depression

Postnatal depression maybe identified as a more common phenomenon in individualistic, as compared to collectivistic societies.

The reasons include biological, hormonal, psychological, social and socioeconomic features.

The psychological distress maybe related to a genetic overlay, or a difficult past, psychological history.

Additionally, unhelpful personality traits, schemas or core beliefs, may compound the problem.

Pregnancy and parenthood are joyful life events for most couples.

However, these events demand additional planning and delegation of resources, to alleviate associated stress.

The difficulties maybe related to unreasonable and unrealistic expectations, from the self, or the significant other in the relationship.

Caring for the newborn includes additional demands, including approximately four hourly feeding patterns, and diaper changes.

Sleep deprivation is a common problem and sheer physical exhaustion can be daunting.

Often the expectation of self to manage the situation adequately can create self-doubt.

The parent that stays at home and is the sole primary caregiver, may experience increasing isolation, and associated resentment.

There may be concern or grief at the loss, or postponement, of coveted and cherished career goals.

The lack of ME time and US time may increase the sense of rift, from significant others.

In some sense, it is also a loss of identity, as an individual, who has experienced the freedom and free will of a self-enhancing individual, to an individual, with a very demanding routine.

Additionally, there may be increasing pressure on the parent, that provides the financial support, to opt for longer working hours, where expenses have increased, and the cash flow income possibly halved.

Working late hours may add to the overall family resentment and increased feelings of isolation and monotony, of unshared home tasks.

In addition to working longer hours, the expectation of support in the care of the infant and help with home chores, maybe an exhaustive effort.

Providing the necessary emotional support, to one another, may be difficult, at times.

Having other children to care for, or pets, may add to the increasing stress and psychological distress, experienced as postpartum/postnatal depression.

The joy of having children can, however, be sustainable, via adequate realistic appraisals and realistic expectations.

Rest, rejuvenation and respite are necessary considerations, in various scenarios.

Again, many models prevail to manage this event of childbirth, that is a very significant life event, for most couples.

In the first model, the care of the infant and mother, is divided between many significant others, mainly grandparents, providing adequate rest and respite.

The grandparents may opt to stay with the couple, for geographical or other convenience reasons, for a period of time, within the postpartum.

There may be further ongoing assistance with home help, cooking, groceries and care of the older children or pets.

Predictability in routines and informed delegation of roles, is preferred over uncertainty.

Regular rituals and interludes are included in the process, alleviating isolation and creating an atmosphere of joy and care.

In this model, issues like setting boundaries, overzealous grandparents, excessive visitors and a difficult baby or mother temperament, may complicate the issues.

However, empathic communication and adequate belief in infant mother attachment, could resolve some of the issues.

The role of a secure attachment, between the parents and the newborn infant, is the predominant priority.

Within this secure attachment, with the primary caregivers, the infant can flourish with other significant caregivers, who provide additional love, affection, attention and respite. The infant then returns back to the bonding and security, of the primary parent caregivers.

Secure attachment enhancing activities, with primary parent caregivers, may include feeding and nurturing the infant, bathing and bedtime storytelling rituals and other play and sing along activities.

Feeding and nurturing includes engaging and communicating with the awake infant.

This is without distraction of the television or other media and is encouraged towards adequate infant-parent bonding, and a secure attachment.

However, the parent couple is also encouraged to focus on some ME time and US time, without experiencing guilt and self-doubt, about being good parents.

The couple maybe encouraged to have some respite, such as a quiet scenic drive, shopping, self-care or dining out, or other such fulfilling activities.

This helps with the monotony and isolation of nurturing and changing diapers, in extended sequence.

Secure attachment between the infant and the primary caregivers, makes the respite provided by significant other caregivers, seem like a win-win situation.

Often, the realisation that two individuals may have had to manage a routine, that is made easier, by the support of, additional, two to four supportive grandparents, is relieving.

Additionally, an important career choice is return to work, after childbirth.

Return to work and maternal and paternal leave, is the choice of the parent couple, and a personal decision, based on many associated factors.

Early return to career goals maybe assisted by ongoing support from extended family, often facilitated by geographical convenience.

In the second model, the expectation is that the couple manage the childbirth, and postpartum process, without any or minimal family involvement.

This characteristic maybe related to an unrealistic expectations of the self or the couple, related to the concept of autonomy.

In this model, there is an increasing, and often premature demand, for very early childcare assistance.

Additional support may be required from local and community mothers groups, and other such facilities.

However, this model may have a higher association, with postpartum depression, and the associated negative experiences.

The problem could be resolvable in some instances, via family support.

Asking parents for help and support, is often associated with difficulties, related to a sense of emotional insecurity, low self-esteem, excessive guarding of autonomy and self-doubt, at being labelled as inadequate, or as being a bad parent.

Feelings of guilt maybe related to previous history with the family, and expectations and interpretations of events.

Hesitancy about the parental response and reaching conclusions, without adequate communication, does not help with the situation.

Often engaging back with their children, as grandparents, and being the required support network, is a possible source of joy, for many empty nesters.

Often grandparents may reminisce happily about the joy they experienced, as parents.

Often grandparents, both paternal and maternal, may learn to work together, as a team, with the common goal of supporting the new parents, and the wonderful bundle of joy that they find in their grandchild.

The third model is related to increasing reliance on nannies, home help and service providers, to assist with the event of a childbirth.

This model is, however, not the most common model from a demographical perspective.

Incidentally, there may be some level of overlap, within the previous models, with some home help and some reliance on other service providers.

Care of the elderly within the family

There are various models, in relation to the care of the elderly, within the family set-up. This immediately includes the care of the ageing parents.

All the models, prevail within the framework of geographical complexity, time constraints, individual temperament, aptitude and priority.

Contentious issues may be related to unfulfilled expectations or unfair, arbitrary management, of roles and responsibilities.

As children move out, to further education and career opportunities, this creates a sense of loneliness and emptiness for parents.

However, this may also be a time for parents to focus on other goals, such as travel, increased involvement in the profession, development of meaningful hobbies, increased involvement and engagement with extended family and friends.

Often, when children get married, or are engaged in a defacto relationship, they would move out of the parental home, in most cultures.

Parents and children may meet on weekends, or special events during the year, such as anniversaries, birthdays or festive occasions.

This could be as part of the ME time, or more specifically, the extended family time.

Having grandchildren, may increase the re-engagement with children, supporting children during their parenthood, in very many ways.

The advantages of the collectivistic approach to families, are inherent in the associated help of grandparents, in the upbringing of grandchildren, sharing of household chores within the family, social support and financial credibility of inheritance from early adulthood.

Other advantages may include privacy to spend some quality time with the spouse or support, towards maintaining career goals.

Further, traditionally, childcare and aged care were a family prerogative, rather than a social, political or fiscal concern.

The family was responsible for the care of ageing parents and family estates.

The advantages are seen as potentially healthy, if perceived from a mature pattern, of emotional and psychological perspective.

The values of mutual tolerance, sustainability and the overarching bigger picture, are paramount.

The perceived disadvantages of living with parents,

after marriage, are the sense of unfairness and the expectation to change and adapt on occasion, marginalisation, alienation and isolation, the feeling of lack of control over child upbringing, or family finances.

There may be unreasonable division of family chores and assets, unfulfilled expectations of privacy, feelings of lack of autonomy, excessive authoritarianism and the belief in perfection.

The associated belief is that problems cannot be resolved via mutual communication or demarcation in roles and responsibilities.

The expectations based on individualism ideology rather than collectivism, social pressure, peer pressure or contradictory parental pressure and demands, is unhelpful.

Unhealthy emotions including jealousy, pettiness, anxiety and sadness, compound the issues.

The harmony can be perpetuated into healthy family and extended family, with the children in the family, attaining an healthy social perspective.

The disharmony can lead to an angry couple that may eventuate into extra marital relationships, divorce or embittered domestic violence.

Additional issues, like health concerns, drug and alcohol problems or oblivion to the requirements of the next person, may undermine family unity.

The above discussion again, maybe perceived across various models.

In the first model, the care of the elderly or ageing parents, is the responsibility of the sons and daughters, within the family. This maybe, as part of the joint family.

Expectations, related to the traditional system of the son taking care of elderly parents, may also prevail.

Hence, the first model maybe subject to some essential conflict, as to the preferential issues, in the care of the paternal versus maternal, elderly grandparents.

In this instance, convenience and availability of assets, may prevail.

However, it is more likely, that a second model would gain consideration.

In the second model, parents may continue to prefer to live separately, and the married couple would live independently, as a nuclear family.

Geographical proximity maybe considered a matter of convenience.

The parents may choose to downsize in accommodation, sharing the family assets with the children, or to focus on their own lifestyle and interests.

The concept of the granny flat is cohesive with this model, especially with more senior parents or ageing parents.

This is especially helpful in alleviating social isolation, experienced by single, widowed or divorced parents, who may not have re-partnered for very many reasons.

Involvement with family and children and grandchildren, is maintained and encouraged, within the framework of cohesiveness and independence.

The couple may, independently, share their time with both set of parents, as extended family time, alternatively.

Individuals may also spend some ME time, with individual parents, as well.

The maternal and paternal grandparents engage harmoniously on common occasions, especially occasions related to grandchildren, and festive occasions.

In the third model, the couple may decide that time constraints prevent engagement with the in-laws, and each individual takes care of their own parent responsibility.

Grandchildren may or may not get a fair share of time, equally, with both set of grandparents.

The fourth model is related to the care of elderly, as a social and political phenomenon.

The care of the elderly is relegated to retirement villages and aged care homes.

This model has the additional advantage, where individuals with similar interests, may have additional facilities, related to hobbies.

Activities such as community outings, organised card games like Bridge, outdoor and indoor sports, arts, and musical activities, libraries and dining facilities, are acknowledged provisions.

The aged care that includes high dependency, for medical reasons, includes aged care nursing homes, and other options.

Whilst this model fulfills many social needs, especially for the single, divorced or widowed individuals, the model is better conceptualised, within the framework of the family situation.

Loneliness and social isolation, continue to create psychological difficulties like geriatric depression and other demoralising issues for the elderly.

This is one of the more serious problems related to model four, where aged care is delegated, solely, to the social and political system.

Technology may help resolve some communication issues and alleviate social isolation.

However, technology may not replace sharing a

home cooked meal together or playing a board game, together.

It would be a meritorious social obligation, to have grandparents engage with family and grandchildren, over a meal or two, over the week, with some weekends together with family and grandchildren.

Festive occasions, birthdays and anniversaries, entailing family unity, are certainly endorsed, as worthwhile.

It seems and is a possibility that sometimes, women have an overreaction against traditional roles, and models fostering family peace, harmony and unity.

Additionally, individuals may seem to deviate from traditional family roles, that are inclusive of both sides of the family, within the couple dyad.

Whilst gender equality and modern gender roles are worth advocacy, one may also consider this, within the framework of the care of the elderly, within the family.

Change of city, state and country are additional geographical concerns, contradicting aged care, within the family setup.

Migration and citizenship of different countries can be heartbreaking. One can often see, freely weeping senior citizens, at many international airports.

In counties like the United States of America, green cards and citizenships are freely available, to parents of migrants and naturalised American citizens, with a small waiting period.

This humane approach is the most caring, for the needs of grandparents.

However, there are other issues involved here, such as high costs of health insurance, limited social security, and of course a high cost of living.

The system additionally, in the United States of America, however, does not favour easy migration for siblings.

Families are often torn apart and living on two or three different continents.

Contention and hesitation may also include the choice of whose parents get priority in migration.

Often paternal and maternal grandparents may alternate visits, and could be heavily invested in providing childcare, for their working sons and daughters.

However, restrictions on length of stay are truly devastating, at times, to the family support system.

Parents arriving to help the pregnant daughter or daughters-in-law, is a common scenario.

The increasing rate of postnatal depression, is certainly alleviated, in this scenario.

Men and women get back to the workforce with peace of mind, and adequate support from family.

However, government caps to non-citizen grandparent stay, and a negative attitude towards grandparent intention to stay longer, may add to inherent difficulties, within this support system.

Often individuals who are apt at retaining collegiate balance and delegation of roles and responsibilities, within the workforce, may find difficulty in employing the same skills, in the household.

It is definitely possible to maintain family harmony in families, that include extended families.

Setting boundaries and maintaining privacy are an integral part of emotional intelligence.

Independence within cohesiveness can often be fostered by concepts like the granny flat, twin houses, or a shared geographical location.

Adequate secure attachments, a sense of self-worth and self-esteem, can make families a happy and pleasant experience.

Adequate delegation of roles and responsibilities, open communication and family conferences, empathy and respect are the key phenomenon, related to family harmony.

Possible expected acculturation and the difficulties in

maintaining healthy family ties, can have a negative influence, on the systematic process.

Often media caricature, denies family status and family obligations.

Senior citizens are a butt of crude jokes and cruelty, denying hardworking individuals the respite of respect and love, in declining years.

Acculturation, that is accepted within the polarised framework, is not necessarily healthy, psychologically.

Accepting certain values of the migrant nation, whilst retaining family values and roles and responsibilities, fosters the family unity.

Acculturation may also challenge traditional roles.

For example, if the son propagates his traditional role, as the carer of his parents, gender equality demands that the daughter-in-law's parents are also taken into consideration.

In this process, often, one falls into the trap of neglecting responsibility, towards ageing parents, relegating them to model four.

There may be increasing reliance on other family members and neighbours, to provide a supportive role to individuals, who have opted migration out of the country of birth.

Trying to impose model four (in the country of birth) on every migrant family, by making immigration and visas as difficult as possible, is a trauma and challenge to the naturalised workforce, within the migrant country.

In effect, family unity, family harmony, family support and family obligations are an individual responsibility, a family responsibility, a social responsibility and a political responsibility.

Progress needs to be made, on every front, should psychological and emotional health be considered a priority, within the psychosocial environment.

Worksheet Homemaker roles

Homemaker roles	Frequency and hours required	Delegation
Home maintenance		
Vacuuming		
Care of flooring		
Maintaining ensuites		
Dusting		
Making grocery list		
Purchasing groceries		
Lunch boxes		
Stacking groceries		
Cooking routine food		

Other specific issues

Cooking delicacies		
Storing food		
Dishwashing		
Unloading dishwasher		
Cleaning benchtop		
Cleaning stovetop		
Laundry washing		
Laundry drying		
Laundry folding		
Ironing		
Stacking clothes in closets		
Giveaways		
Child Playtime		
Child Storytime		
Child Naptime		
Child Bathing		
Child Feeding		
Dropping the children to daycare/school		
Picking up the children from daycare/school		
Dropping and picking up the children from playdates or extracurricular activities		
Helping children with homework		
Buying gifts		
Planning for special events		
Care of the elderly		
Garden maintenance		
Lawn mowing		

Shovelling snow		
Care of pets		
Doctor appointments		

The list is endless ....

Me time	Activities as an individual	Hobbies

Us time	Activities as a couple	Romantic interludes

Activities as a family	Parents and children

Activities as extended family	Including grandparents

Social activities	Including other family and friends (may overlap with Me time or family time).

Worksheet Assets Management A=B

A Total income of the month

B Expenses of the month as divided between the four individuals of a family of four that includes two children

I 1 Individual 1

I 2 Individual 2

C 1 Child

C2 Child

References

Prochaska JO. Redding CA Evers K. The Transtheoretical Model and Stages of Change. In K. Glanz, B.K. Rimer & F.M. Lewis, (Eds.) Health Behavior and Health Education: Theory, Research, and Practice (3rd Ed.). San Francisco, CA: Jossey-Bass, Inc.2002.

Beck AT. Love is Never Enough. HarperPerrenial, New York, United States of America. 1988.

Deshmukh VM. Toelle BG. Usherwood T. O'Grady B. Jenkins CR. Anxiety, panic and adult asthma: a cognitive-behavioral perspective. Respiratory Medicine. 101(2):194-202, 2007 Feb.

Deshmukh VM. Toelle BG. Usherwood T. O'Grady B. Jenkins CR. The association of comorbid anxiety and depression with asthma-related quality of life and symptom perception in adults. Respirology. 13 (5): 695-702, 2008 Jul.

Abstracts and Presentations

World Congress of Behavioural and Cognitive therapy - July 2019 - Berlin Germany - Poster Presentation

Deshmukh VM. Relationships and Couples Dynamics Within the Stages of Change model: Theoretical Considerations and Application of the Stages of Change Model Within Relationship Dyads.

World Congress of Behavioural and Cognitive therapy - June 2016 - Melbourne Australia - Paper Presentation

Deshmukh VM. Chronic medical conditions and intervention: Case study

World Congress of Behavioural and Cognitive therapy - July 2013 - Lima Peru - Paper Presentation

Deshmukh VM. Advances in our Understanding of the Response to a Stressor.

Australian Association of Cognitive Behaviour Therapy - October 2012 - Sanctuary Cove - Paper Presentation

Deshmukh VM. Advances in our Understanding of the Stress Response: Do the Current Terminologies that we use and our Psychometric Measures Capture these Recent Advances?

American Thoracic Society International Conference-Toronto - May 2008 - Poster Presentation

Evaluation of a psychological intervention in adults with anxiety and asthma targeting asthma-related quality of life. American Journal of Respiratory and Critical Care Medicine. 2008.

Thoracic Society of Australia and New Zealand Annual Scientific Meetings -Melbourne - March 2008 - Poster Presentation

Deshmukh VM. Toelle BG. Usherwood T. O'Grady B. Jenkins CR.

Evaluation of a psychological intervention in adults with anxiety and asthma targeting asthma-related quality of life. Respirology. 2008; 13: A40.

Thoracic Society of Australia and New Zealand Annual Scientific Meetings-Auckland - March 2007- Poster Presentation

Deshmukh VM. Toelle BG. Usherwood T. O'Grady B. Jenkins CR.

The impact of comorbid anxiety on asthma-related quality of life in adults. Respirology. 2007; 12: A39.

American Thoracic Society International Conference - San Francisco - May 2007-Poster Presentation

Deshmukh VM. Toelle BG. Usherwood T. O'Grady B. Jenkins CR.

The impact of comorbid anxiety on asthma-related quality of life in adults. American Journal of Respiratory and Critical Care Medicine. 2007; 175: A61.

Australian Psychological Society Annual Conference - Brisbane - September 2007-Paper Presentation

Deshmukh VM. Toelle BG. Usherwood T. O'Grady B. Jenkins CR. Anxiety, panic and adult asthma: a cognitive-behavioural perspective. Australian Journal of Psychology. 2007. 59: 260.

Australian Association of Cognitive Behavioural Therapy Conference - Surfers Paradise - October 2007- Paper Presentation

Deshmukh VM. Toelle BG. Usherwood T. O'Grady B. Jenkins CR. Anxiety, panic and adult asthma: a cognitive-behavioural perspective.

Australasian College of Emergency Medicine- Winter Symposium- Launceston- August 2007- Paper Presentation

Deshmukh VM. Toelle BG. Usherwood T. O'Grady B. Jenkins CR. The impact of comorbid anxiety on asthma-related quality of life in adults.

Asia Pacific Society of Respiratory Medicine Conference- December 2007- Gold Coast-Poster Presentation

Deshmukh VM. Toelle BG. Usherwood T. O'Grady B. Jenkins CR. Association between anxiety, asthma quality of life and frequent emergency department visits in adults with asthma

Disclaimer

This piece of creative work is a social treatise.

Some aspects of this treatise are based on research. Some references can be provided for the research basis of this treatise.

However, the predominant perspective is based on clinical and social experience, as a Clinical Psychologist.

Dr. Vandana Deshmukh has been living in Sydney, Australia for twenty-two years. She has been practicing as a Clinical Psychologist for eighteen years (@ publication of the book).

The issues discussed are most relevant to the process of acculturation.

However, the issues, that are delineated in this treatise are universal, to most couples and families, and organisations, to a lesser or greater extent.

This treatise should be used in conjunction with professional advice, at all times.

The author acknowledges that some, or many of the concepts, outlined above, are idealistic, in principle.

However, implementing them in tangible practice, is intricate.

This is often fraught with complexities, interpersonal conflicts and contradictions, requiring individualisation with collaborative, delicate, neutral and informed therapeutic management, maintaining consistency and patience.